**Lillie was a goddess
Lillie was a whore**

Previous Publications from Penelope Scambly Schott

Novel
A Little Ignorance

Fictional Memoir
Rumi and Lily: An Internet Love Story (with Jean Anaporte's dog)

Poetry Chapbooks
My Grandparents Were Married for Sixty-five Years
These Are My Same Hands
Almost Learning to Live in This World
Wave Amplitude in the Mona Passage
Aretha's Hat (with Kathryn Stripling Byer)
Lovesong for Dufur

Poetry Collections
The Perfect Mother
Baiting the Void
May the Generations Die in the Right Order
Six Lips
Crow Mercies

Narrative Poetry
Penelope: The Story of the Half-Scalped Woman
The Pest Maiden: A Story of Lobotomy
A is for Anne: Mistress Hutchinson Disturbs the Commonwealth

Lillie was a goddess
Lillie was a whore

Penelope Scambly Schott

Mayapple Press 2013

© Copyright 2013 by Penelope Scambly Schott

Published by   MAYAPPLE PRESS
                 362 Chestnut Hill Rd.
                 Woodstock, NY 12498
                 www.mayapplepress.com

ISBN 978-1-936419-25-8

ACKNOWLEDGMENTS

Little Patuxent Review, "According to the Escort Agency's Calendar, November Is Manatee Awareness Month"

Radius, "craigslist"

Roar Magazine, "Liesl in Queens, New York City, 1965"

Tawdry Bawdry, "He Nicknames what He Loves and Takes It Out to Dance," "My First Divorce"

US 1 Worksheets, "From Easternmost Oregon to the Steens Mountain Round-Up"

VoiceCatcher, "In which this Wife Tells Her Husband the Truth about Sex in Marriage"

Cover art by Penelope Scambly Schott. Cover designed by Judith Kerman. Book designed and typeset by Amee Schmidt with titles in Myriad Pro and text in Georgia. Author photo courtesy of Mr. Dalpatbhai in the ruins of Dholavira, Gujarat, India.

Contents

Part One: Prostitutes in the History of the World

In the Beginning, Prostitutes Were Sacred	9
Walking around with it every day of my life	10
Male and Female He Created Them	11
My First Divorce	12
What Is This Thing Called Love?	13
Why Lillie Became a Prostitute—version one	14
What She Said	15
Patience on the Flower Boat	16
Why a Happily Married Man Would Go to a Prostitute	17
He Nicknames What He Loves and Takes It Out to Dance	18
The Life of Saint Gregory, 3rd Century Bishop of Neocaesarea	19
Virgin Mary, Protector of Whores, Pray for Me	20
*Un*people	21
My Friend's Story	22
What 27% of the male population is doing right now	23
Within the Standard Marital Contract	24
Thumb-Indexed Alphabetized Blue Book for the Sporting Man-about-Town	25
My intercourse with these women	26
"Spend a Night with Venus, and then a Lifetime with Mercury"	28
Why Lillie Became a Prostitute—version two	29
My Lover is the Ceiling	30

Part Two: Lillie in the American Wild West

A Folk History of the 1849 California Gold Rush and Subsequent Prostitute Rush	33
Why Lillie Became a Prostitute—version three	34
Miss Lillie Reports on Society and Culture in San Francisco during the Gold Rush	35
My Monkey in his Dear Little Green-striped Shirt	36
Why Lillie Became a Prostitute—version four	37
"And how are you gentlemen on this fine fall evening?"	38
Lillie Used to Eat Oatmeal with Fresh Cream	39
All Last Week, Business was Slow	40
Lillie Departs San Francisco	41
The Lay of the Land	42
The Owls' Sacred Book of Hours	43

Why Lillie Became a Prostitute—version five	45
Miss Lillie Finds Portland Wet and Hypocritical	46
From Easternmost Oregon to the Steens Mountain Round-up	47
Miss Lillie Becomes a Regular Traveler	48
Lake County Desert, Oregon	52
In this high desert place of ill repute	53
If You Want to Make the Money, You Gotta Go Where They're At	54
Miss Lillie Finally Retires Back in Portland	55

Part Three: Nothing New Under the Sun

Prostitution and Sanitation in Portland, Oregon	59
Lilah's Learning Curve	60
Soiled Doves	62
Liesl in Queens, New York City, 1965	63
The German Lilli Cartoon Becomes the American Barbie doll	64
Automatic On-Line Translation from a Foreign Text I Can No Longer Locate on the Internet	65
Why Lillie Became a Prostitute—version six	66
After Great Pain	67
Making the Beast with Two Backs, or how to be more vulgar than Iago	68
How to Deal with SWBS	69
In which the wife serves as the husband's emergency equipment	71
craigslist	72
Tick-Tock, Time to Fuck	75
The Prostitute with the Heart of Gold	76
The Classifieds Celebrate our Savior's Birth, Alleluia	77
Why Lillie Became a Prostitute—version seven	78
Cosmetics, from *kosm'tikos*, skilled in arranging	79
In which this wife tells her husband the truth about sex in marriage	80
According to the Escort Agency's Calendar, November Is Manatee Awareness Month	81
Deathless Aphrodite of the Spangled Mind	82
About the Author	83
Bibliography	84

Buy this Book

Writing is like prostitution.
First we do it for love.
Then we do it for a few friends.
Then we do it for money.

—Molière

The lily is a symbol of innocence and purity as well as beauty.

—www.thinkbabynames.com

Sex work is the place where the great powers of our culture—sex and money—come together.

—Drew Campbell in Whores and Other Feminists, *ed. Jill Nagle, 1997*

Lily understood that beauty is only the raw material of conquest and that to convert it to success, other arts are required.

—Edith Wharton, The House of Mirth, *1905*

It is merely a question of degree whether a woman sells herself to one man, in or out of marriage, or to many men.

—Emma Goldman, 1917

For the sisterhood—those who know and those who want to understand

Note:

Although the following material is based on research, some of the female characters—including nineteenth-century Miss Lillie of the American West—are fictionalized composites, while others speak in their own voices.

Part One: Prostitutes in the History of the World

In the Beginning, Prostitutes Were Sacred

> *My vulva, the horn*
> *The Boat of Heaven..*
>   —*from* Hymn of Inanna

Sex, our first sacrament and blessing—
ask the hummingbird, ask the humming clover,
the lovers of the world loving this world

into being. Before we knew how babies
happened, woman-magic brought them forth,
miraculous as Mary's virgin conception.

Praise the Great Mother in her transformations—
she has always been, will always be with us.
Praise her. Say it, sing it, *Praise her now*.

Inanna who brings the crops to fruit
Inanna who fills rivers with monthly sacred blood
Inanna who lends the power of thrones

and also her tempting handmaid Lilitu,
Ishtar of Iruk, town of sacred courtesans,
Qadshu, the Great Whore of Canaan,

convents of women singing the hours,
the daughters dancing those dark hours
as they safely carry the sun boat of Ra,

Aphrodite's thousand temple harlots,
perfumed devadasis in Hindu shrines—
all sacred women of night, *praise them*.

I am singing the vulva, source of creation,
the genital waters, the harlot-place,
the holy place, the permanent Mother.

What lies inside the lily lies inside me.

Walking around with it every day of my life

Living grotto

Secret source

Earth's center

First home

Concupiscent indent

Hollowness

Sinkhole

Twat

Insidious concavity

The filthy place

Crevasse

Abyss

Male and Female He Created Them

Female and Male She created them
female and male someone created Them
female and male something created them

how amoebas split into the same amoeba
how mixing two can create a third thing
how only sex makes us mix our DNA

how in male mammals
someone hung the apparatus
out to dangle, out to beg

to insist, to insert, to manufacture
out of need, out of rapture
more of itself

female and male She created them
female and male in Her own body
female and male She will create

male and female
I have created them
Oh, my daughter, my son

Hi, kids—love ya!

My First Divorce

We agreed to it the night before
then went to bed as if nothing had changed.

All night I dreamed about money
and what our children ate.

Come morning,
I climbed on top of him

with the desperate vigor
of an amateur whore.

>Dearest sisters in the trade,
>I sucked it up.

>*Lillie was a temptress, Lillie was a snake.*
>*When I got to Lillie's house,*
>*she knew how to fake.*

What Is This Thing Called Love?

> *When he finally got inside me,*
> *I think it went on for a few minutes.*
> *—quote taken from Ashly Lorenzana,*
> Sex, Drugs & Being an Escort

I've seen how the horse does it, and dogs.
Does the bitch want it? Or the mare?

A snail does it to itself. How can that be?
Or is it, any snail can do any other snail?

I saw a young man who was so beautiful
that I wanted to touch him. Or did I want

him to touch me? When I first felt desire,
I thought I was getting sick. After that,

I knew what it was and I wanted it again.
I found the hole where a man could go in.

Or a finger. But what I don't understand
is calling this *Love*.

Why Lillie Became a Prostitute—version one

Because Father was a preacher
Because Father said we are all born sinners
Because I liked to make up tales
        about those red chickens
Because I lied about the lost velvet ribbon
Because Mother's house was immaculate
Because when I was ten she died of overwork
Because my good sister bled to death in childbirth
Because Father pronounced me *damned*

What She Said

> *"How do the names of the words work, she said"*
> *—from "Landscape of the Husked"*
> *by James Grinwis*

She said, I am a prostitute

She said, I am a whore

She said, I am invisible

She said, I am a sorceress

She said, I am a crocodile

She said, I am a public servant

She said, my name is *pig swill*

and I am a drilled rock

Patience on the Flower Boat

On the Pearl River in Canton,
gentlemen gather for the evening:
a fine supper, music, and a girl a piece

With a virgin of 13, he tries the flower
If she is 14, he may cultivate the flower
Now she is 15, and he gathers the flower

on the slow Pearl River
on the Flower Boat
on and on

Lillie was a hooker, Lillie was a fish.
When I set sail on Lillie's boat,
she granted every wish.

Why a Happily Married Man Would Go to a Prostitute

If a man has a wet dream, Lilith laughs

The daughters of Lilith, those demon Night-hags,
so expert at making love—

after one night with a daughter of Lilith, no man
can be satisfied with a mortal woman.

*Hey, man, you know how it goes.
I really do love my wife*

*and I respect her so I can't ask her to...
Man, you didn't see me here.*

---

*Lillie was her knockers, Lillie was her snatch.
When I knocked at Lillie's house,
she lifted up the latch.*

He Nicknames What He Loves and Takes It Out to Dance

Ass candle
Battering ram
Crotch cobra
Divining rod
Eel
Fool sticker
Giggle stick
Hair splitter
Irish root
Joy stick
Kosher pickle
Lizard
Mister Bluevein
Nine-inch knocker
One-eyed pants mouse
Pump handle
Quim wedge
Rumpleforeskin
Sweet thumb of love
Tummy banana
Uncle Johnson
Vanquisher
Whore pipe
Xylophone hammer
Yum-yum
Zucchini

> Now I've said my *ABC's*,
> tell me what you think of me.

The Life of Saint Gregory, 3rd Century Bishop of Neocaesarea

Gregory Thaumaturgus *wonder-worker*
could drive out demons.

This good Saint Gregory
was accused by a prostitute of not paying her.

This holy Saint Gregory
denied he had used the woman,

but he paid her anyhow—

whereupon
she was immediately possessed by a demon.

Which parts of this saint story
don't you believe?

> *Lillie was an incubus, Lillie was a demon.*
> *When I went to Lillie's house,*
> *I shot her full of semen.*

Virgin Mary, Protector of Whores, Pray for Me

In a medieval convent beside a forest
somewhere in Germany,
a nun named Beatrix once ran away
with her pagan lover.

When she returned fifteen years later,
nobody had realized
that good Sister Beatrix was missing
because the Virgin Mary,

full of grace and protector of whores,
had served in her place.
Only the oak trees of the old forest
ever noticed,

clutching their brown leaves in prayer.

Lillie was redemption, Lillie was my sin.
When I came to Lillie's house,
she always let me in.

*Un*people

> *...for all men, girls, and parts of girls, are unpeople.*
> *—quotes taken from Alex Comfort,*
> The Joy of Sex, *1972*

Ladies, didn't we know this?

How our breasts
are two plump whores
gallivanting down the street
with a wobble?

How our twinned buttocks
do an up-and-down dance
we shall never witness?

How our moist pink lips
whisper?

And yet men resent us
because they need us,

because they fear us,
because they fear
becoming us.

> *The vagina*
> *looks like a castrating wound*
> *and bleeds regularly.*
>
> *It swallows the penis*
> *and regurgitates it*
> *limp.*

Poor little Alex. He does need comfort.

My Friend's Story

Her young husband required sex every night.
She was out one evening at a pre-birth class.
He went into their bedroom and masturbated
and dropped his sticky Kleenex on the carpet
for her to pick up. Sex in marriage is sacred.

What 27% of the male population is doing right now

1. Some of the terms starting with the letter *B*:

bashing the candle
bleeding the weasel
buffing the banana
bopping the baloney
burping the worm

2. or if you find rhyme sublime:

flogging the log
jerkin' the gherkin
pounding your flounder
wonking your cronker

3. or you wish to be wordy, verbose, and prolix:

increasing the surface temperature of your ship's main cannon by means of rapid linear motion

God bless the Working Girls who save men from manual labor

Within the Standard Marital Contract

He unbuttoned his pressed shirt
and hung it over their bedroom chair.
He folded his suit pants along the crease.
Keys clinked and fell to the floor.
Neatly, he tucked back their top sheet.

Almost naked, she took off her socks
and rolled them into expensive shoes,
right into right, left into left.
She set the shoes neatly side by side
under the dust ruffle of their bed.

A drape scalloped the icy window
where flakes drifted like enchanted fish
through the slow tide of hemlocks,
and the long rhododendron leaves
closed up tight like clam shells.

Their groomed dog pranced into the room
clamping between perfect white teeth
a gristly half-chewed bone—
the bone's inside full of marrow clumps,
its outside streaked with dried blood.

As he circled uncalloused fingertips
around and around her chilled nipples,
she thought of swirls in cinnamon bread.
They were going to do this thing again.
She checked it off the calendar of her mind.

Thumb-Indexed Alphabetized Blue Book for the Sporting Man-about-Town

Where might he go tonight? Let's look.
His damp thumb flips through his book:

*A*cademy of Venus
*B*ang house
*C*athouse
*D*ame house
*E*scort agency
*F*uckery
*G*rinding house
*H*og ranch
*I*rish clubhouse
*J*uke house
*K*nocking-joint
*L*adies' boardinghouse
*M*assage parlor
*N*aughty house
*O*yster bed
*P*oontang palace
*Q*uick stop
*R*ed-lighterie
*S*porting house
*T*ittery
*U*pstairs parlor
*V*aulting school
*W*ank house
X-rated establishment
*Y*es house
*Z*ipper zoo

Whichever you pick, Mister,
have a nice evening. Sir.

My intercourse with these women

> *—quoted from* My Secret Life, *no date,
> privately printed by "Walter"*

*makes me think
what a godsend
having a cunt is
to many women,
who would starve
without it.*

      Wow, what a meal ticket.
      Why didn't I think of it?

*And what a comfort
that is to men who,
if they couldn't get
a cheap fuck,
must frig themselves
or bugger each other.*

      Well, we can't be having that,
      can we?

*But surely, the seed
in a man's testicles
will and must
come out
by some process
natural or unnatural.*

      It's the hydraulic aspect of physics,
      isn't it?

*To their class I owe
a debt of gratitude:
they have been
my refuge in sorrow,*

*they have saved me
from drink, gambling,
and perhaps worse.*

    Oh, Walter, how tragic.
    We just hate to imagine.

    But the Lord has blessed you
    and you have been rescued.

    Aren't you lucky,
    you cheap little fucker?

---

    *Lillie was my savior, Lillie was my shame.
    When I called at Lillie's house,
    I gave a made-up name.*

"Spend a Night with Venus, and then a Lifetime with Mercury"

1

Chancre: first manifestation of syphilis,
     a dull-red, hard, genital lesion

Cauterization: with a red-hot iron
     Sinners get what they deserve:
     demons in Hell with glowing pokers.
     Oops, no, that was the Doctor.

Mercurial ointment:
     Until your teeth hurt
     until your gums bleed
     until you get ulcers in the mouth
     until you get gangrene of the jaw
     until you die of mercury poisoning

2

Or, because there are periods of latency, any folk cure
can seem to work. Mr. Peddler, want a quick buck
off someone else's rotten luck?
Consider peddling one of these:
     Armenian Pills
     *Bursted's Gleet Cure (Gleet, from ME glet = slime or
     mucous)*
     Drovett's French Lunar Pills
     Lafayette Mixture
     Naples Soap
     Ore Cinnabar
     Potassium Iodide
     Red Drops
     Silver Nitrate (injected directly into the urethra)
     The Unfortunate's Friend

3

Penicillin? Sorry, dearies. Not yet.

Why Lillie Became a Prostitute—version two

Because we were orphans
and my two baby brothers were starving
Their eyes got huge and then turned dull
I was only going to do it once
Their little hands trembled
as they bit at the crusts

> *Lillie was holy, Lillie was haunted.*
> *When I called at Lillie's house,*
> *she gave me what I wanted.*

My Lover is the Ceiling

The ceiling is my lover
I gaze into its cracked plaster
I am transfixed
by yellowed ivory paint

*I look unto heaven
whence cometh my salvation*
Sometimes I don't remember
which man sweats on top of me

When I was a child
in a pressed white pinafore
I lay on the cool lawn
watching clouds float

Above my head
the clouds flipped below me
so I was lying upside down
high over heaven

---

*Lillie was my chapel, Lillie was my Shrine.
Each time I went to Lillie's house,
I drank her in like wine.*

Part Two: Lillie in the American Wild West

A Folk History of the 1849 California Gold Rush and Subsequent Prostitute Rush

The miners came in '49,
  the whores in '51.
They lay down on the barroom floor
  And made the Native Son.

—anonymous

Why Lillie Became a Prostitute—version three

Because he came to the farm with his banjo
Because he had hair like an angel
Because he had eyes like a devil
Because he slept in our barn
Because I went early to milk the cow

Lillie was a banjo, Lillie was a gourd.
When I came to Lillie's house,
I sang out Praise the Lord.

Miss Lillie Reports on Society and Culture in San Francisco during the Gold Rush

When we landed in Frisco, every man in town
tipped his hat, and some of them bowed.
After their good wives arrived from the East,
the same men pretended we didn't exist.
But once the new theater had curtained boxes
they quickly remembered how to talk to us.

My Monkey in his Dear Little Green-striped Shirt

I got him from a sailor who couldn't pay the bill.
The sailor was sorry and waved a slow goodbye.
The monkey watched him walk down the stairs.
I didn't know how you should hold a monkey—
by his little black hand or like you hold a baby—
so I grabbed the collar of the green-striped shirt.
I've never held a baby. When I got knocked up,
the Madam said impatiently, *Go back upstairs
and turn a couple of tricks, and you can pay
for your own damn abortion.*

Why Lillie Became a Prostitute—version four

Because we lived in a remote valley
Because the bare hills hemmed us in
Because only the river went somewhere else
Because I had never seen a real city
and the Bible salesman offered me a ride

"And how are you gentlemen on this fine fall evening?"

In the gas-lit parlor
five young ladies on love seats,
satin evening dresses reflected
in gilt-framed mirrors.
A discreet bell:
Madam opens the paneled door.
Whiffs of cold creep from the hall
where two gentlemen
lift their hats,
unwind their knitted mufflers,
the neatly purled rows worked
by wife or fiancée.
Everyone smiles:
the two brunettes, the redhead,
even platinum Miss Lillie, tossing
her curls like a dare.
A genteel soiree:
nobody mentions money or sex.
But hips touch. A hand wanders.
Corks pop.
Just so much.
Even the most ardent gentleman
cannot perform impaired.
Time is money.
The fellows choose.
The banister up to the second floor
has been polished by sweaty hands.
Discreetly,
let us close
the upstairs bedroom doors.
The peephole looks in, not out.
All under control.

Lillie Used to Eat Oatmeal with Fresh Cream

Our milch cow was named Aurelia May.
When I pressed my cheek to her flank
I heard her cud move from one stomach
into the next.

Now I drink dark whiskey for breakfast
with one raw egg. The six chickens
are good enough layers but nobody here
bothers to name them.

The Champagne our customers order
and pour into crystal goblets in the parlor
tastes like bubbles mixed with spiders
and cold piss.

When the last gentlemen have finished
and I can unstring my bodice and wash
off everything sticky, I lie down to chew
the tips of my bleached hair.

All Last Week, Business was Slow

One gentleman asked, *No new girls?*
The clients prefer somebody fresh.
Our Madam says to pretend I am French—
after lunch we will re-groom my bush.

> *Merci, Madame,*
> *Bon soir, messieurs*

Lillie Departs San Francisco

It's time to put on my travel gown
before I take that first step down

from the top parlor house in Frisco
to a brothel with last year's dishes.

Next stop, the cribs. That's no laugh.
I've seen those girls. Volume traffic.

Skin blotchy from booze. Dirt
under their nails. Their clients

don't take off their boots. No,
Madam so-and-so. I won't do it.

Let her find herself a real Frenchie.
This local trade is getting too picky.

I don't see what Madam means.
I can still pass for nineteen.

Ambitious young women needed,
says the ad. Okay, full speed

ahead to beautiful new Oregon.
My sails are unfurled. I'm gone.

The Lay of the Land

Spare me, says Lillie, from going to sea again.
This was worse than rounding the Horn.
The wide mouth of the Columbia River,
dreadful waves from every direction.

The veiled lady with her wedding ring
who had shunned me the whole trip
grabbed onto my arm. We all expected
to drown, be it quickly, be it now. Never
in my pure or working life have I prayed
so goddamn hard.

They call that town Astoria. I called it
Salvation. Briefly, we tied up.

Then the river smoothed out and the tide
carried us upriver through dense green fog
until we docked at Portland. Stumps.
Nothing but shouting and stumps.

What a stinking, smoky, soggy,
muddy dump.

A man with a barrow picked up my trunk.
Where to? he asked, touching his cap.
My cloak gave scant cover against the rain.

*To the most expensive parlor house in town.
And fast.*

Lord, how that man looked me over.

The Owls' Sacred Book of Hours

How a great horned owl
glides through the trees
behind the parlor house
as Miss Lillie dreams
and a little girl on a swing
stops to watch huge wings
that make no noise
that make no noise
Miss Lillie rises past noon
to preen and groom
to sit in an upstairs window
a laced bodice cut low
she leans toward the street
a ready half-smile to bait
the well-dressed men
passing by and again
She licks rouged lips
and rests a fingertip
on the bosom's curve
no question of nerve
as she tilts her chin
toward the window pane
drops her silk wrapper
unfolds a local paper
Scandal! Scandal!
Fine society is appalled
that town fathers permit
this daily display of tits
to corrupt young men
and pure boys *Amen*
say the church ladies
covering their babies'
owl eyes with white
blankets and tonight
when their good men
need to go out again
in this hour of screech owls
when stray cats yowl

behind the tavern
while home is a haven
for the corseted wives
polishing knives
and forks in the pantry
while the gallantry
of town goes to parley
in the gilded parlor
that lures them upstairs
while the wives' prayers
dissolve into curses
as they dump out purses
to count their egg change
with unconcealed rage
no longer innocent
or feigning ignorance
of the sins of husbands
fall of the tall lustful sons
The barred owl devours
a mouse as the blue hour
silvers while Miss Lillie dumps
her finery on a worn lumpy
feather bed *whoo hoo hoo*
trills the owl and mid-afternoon
Lillie will wake and modestly
re-lace her red satin bodice

Because everything new is old—
how avidly the saw-whet owl
slips into a warm hole

Why Lillie Became a Prostitute—version five

Because the boss at the mill
used to pinch all us girls
Because wages at the mill
never went up
Because my gentleman caller
wasn't a gentleman
and I wanted a church hat
and these white leather gloves

Miss Lillie Finds Portland Wet and Hypocritical

Too much rain. Too much fuss.
My eyes are turning green as moss.

Don't talk to me about reform.
It isn't us. It's the men who come.

Proper Portland is getting too cozy.
The club ladies are planting roses.

What do they say about the West?
You travel to see the elephant.

Someone must be shit-face drunk.
There is no elephant. Just my trunk

and this stagecoach across Oregon.
I have this letter in my gloved hand:

Vale, Oregon. A new frontier.
I'll be Miss Lillie, the pioneer,

heading out where cattle graze.
In a new place, I'll be a new face.

From Easternmost Oregon to the Steens Mountain Round-up

Who knew Oregon was so wide?
It's dry and flat or dry and steep.
Yes, I'm the classiest girl in Vale,
but where are all the men?
Herding cattle, herding sheep.
And here we come after them,
herding men. In canvas tents
we work. Business is steady
up in Whorehouse Meadow.
One of the Basque shepherds
asks me my name. That's all
he can say in his bad English.
He seems as lonesome as I am.

Quite early the next morning
at the dark edge of the meadow,
I come upon him carving *Lili*
into the white bark of an aspen.

> *Lillie was a whisper, Lillie was a moan.*
> *When I went to Lillie's house,*
> *I no longer felt alone.*

Miss Lillie Becomes a Regular Traveler

> When we girls travel in winter,
> Madam calls it *summer vacation*

What Rides in the Covered Wagon

A white iron bedstead
with a set of springs,
a horsehair mattress
and a strip of sailcloth
to keep muddy boots
off clean sheets,
a black wood stove
to heat up the tent,
a galvanized sitz tub
to soak my sore cunt,
an oak washstand
for pitcher and bowl,
two upright chairs
and a brass spittoon,
a high-arched trunk
with iron strapping.

What I Pack in my Trunk

1. Daguerreotypes of my Parents

The hinged double frame
unlocks with a silver hook.
Inside his brown oval
my father's starched collar
holds his head rigid.
In her own chaste oval,
Mother's pleated bosom
swells above her corset.
If a man plans to stay all night
I hook the portraits shut.

2. My Faithful Washbasin and Pitcher

Matching crackle glaze
with a chipped gold edge
and blowsy
hand-painted flowers.
The breakable pitcher and bowl
ride wrapped in my lingerie.

I wash my men gently—
a mother washing
the miniature swollen genitalia
of her very own newborn son.

3. My Great Grandmother's Silver-plated Dressing Table Set

Comb, brush, and mirror:
tortoise shell, boar's bristle,
needle-worked back.
When I was a small child,
my grandma used to announce
they came from Paree-France.

4. Bed Linens and Clothes

I use muslin sheets for work,
and silk when I sleep alone.
Very early in the morning
I tromp to the necessary
in rag-wrapped pin curls
and faded flannel duster.
I own my own whole body
and also the pale dawn sky.

5. My Supply of Cheap Candles

Sometimes it's a four-candle night,
one after another,

because the gentlemen like to see
what they're getting.
I'd just as soon not. The old ones
are ugly, and the young ones
make me think of their mothers
who wouldn't like me.

6. *The Red Lantern*

It hangs from the top
front tent pole.
Everyone knows
what it means.
There's a straight-backed chair
for waiting outside,
and down on the ground,
the brass spittoon.
I let them
take off their hats.

7. *And Last, but not Least, the Derringer*

Small and neatly made,
the handle embossed.
It allows just one shot.
One *accurate* shot.
Yes, ma'am,
I have used it.

What I Hold inside my Body

Seed of strangers,
grunts of strangers,
indifference of strangers,
oblivion of strangers.
gold coins.

What I Try to Hold in my Mind

like cold stars deep in a well:
the pouch of the orchid,
the seamless skin of a dolphin,
the glossy self-sufficiency of cats

> *Lillie was a nomad, Lillie was a cloud.*
> *When I stood outside Lillie's house,*
> *I waited in a crowd.*

Lake County Desert, Oregon

Cross the alkali flats
cross the dried lake
lake as memory
lake as grave
grave for a platted town
grave for a railroad head
head of a new corporation
head in a dream
dream of rain
dream of sheep
sheep pulling bunch grass
sheep and their bones
bones of an empire
bones of wishing
wishing for rain
wishing for storms
storms piling clouds
storms low to the rim
rim of basalt
rim of small caves
caves caked black with soot
caves of ancient sandals
sandals of the dead
sandals of the spirits walking
walking mountain and edge
walking hope and loss
loss of the shearing sheds
loss of the wooden rake
rake the gullies
rake the sage brush
brush your crusted eyes
brush the hair of the whores
whores on Roberta Street
whores for the herders
herders who've lacked for women
herders who pay with silver dollars
dollars we earn on our backs

In this high desert place of ill repute

a black locust tree
spills fragrant tiers
of white blossoms:
a bridal bouquet

  a sweet girl like you
  a smart girl like you
  a pretty girl like you
  a girl like you
               You
  in a place like this?

Dear sanctimonious sir,
have you seen my long thorns?
Where is your flesh most tender?
Where is your skin most thin?
Oh, did you want a virgin?
No problem.
        (All it takes
is one leech or a chip of glass
tucked into the right place,
and I can fool 'em.)

  Lillie was a thistle seed, Lillie was a burr.
  Of all the girls at Lillie's house,
  I was stuck on her.

If You Want to Make the Money, You Gotta Go Where They're At

This new madam likes me
because I'm willing to travel.

But who knew
we would always be moving?

I'm not joking.
We rode all the way up to the Yukon

where a miner dusted
my whole body with gold.

Afterward,
I shook out my sheet and hair

carefully over the bar
so the saloon keeper

could get out his scales
and weigh the gold dust.

Hey, girls, trust me:
travel pays.

Miss Lillie Finally Retires Back in Portland

Suppose Miss Lillie survives to grow old
Suppose she managed to avoid syphilis
Suppose she never resorted to laudanum
Suppose she saved her gold money
Suppose she holds up her silver mirror
and smiles to admire her white hair
Suppose she lives in a warm house
with dark hand-cut woodwork
and pocket doors that glide shut
Suppose she knows another old tart
and the two gals drink tea together
out of transparent Limoges cups
with curly handles, and now and then
on a rainy afternoon they add a dash
of decent whiskey as they sip and nap
Suppose Lillie once had a monkey
and now she keeps two calico cats
who lick her cream pitcher clean
Suppose she has retired in Portland
where she laughs over Nancy Boggs
who runs a floating brothel in the middle
of the Willamette with liquor downstairs
and girls upstairs and how Nancy avoids
liquor fees and fights off police with a hose
Maybe Lillie knows fireplug Liverpool Liz
with her famous four-pound "little bauble"
of diamonds and gold on her bulky bosom
and Miss Lillie lives on until Liz's race track
is bought by the city to be turned into a park
complete with an elegant sunken rose garden

Enough, says Miss Lillie, laying
her powdered face on her lacy pillow
Enough with all this respectability
I think of those fellows, hundreds
or thousands of men, how grateful
they were, how many lives I saved

Part Three: Nothing New Under the Sun

Prostitution and Sanitation in Portland, Oregon

> *If you do away with harlots, the world will be convulsed with lust. Prostitution in towns is like the sewer in a palace; take away the sewers and the palace becomes an impure and stinking place.*
>   *—Thomas Aquinas,* Summa Theologicae, *1265-1274*

City of loggers, city of sailors, city convulsed
with lust, city of rivers, city of stumps, palaces
of congenial females, lush parlors of whores,
how you thrive. Decade after decade of reform,
and nothing changes. The 1864 Portland sewer
was a wooden trench along Montgomery Street
from Fourth Avenue down to the Willamette River,
meant to cleanse this city of roses, city of bridges,
city of used girls waiting on Eighty-second Avenue.

> *Lillie was a corner girl, Lillie was on smack.*
> *When I went to Lillie's house,*
> *she hit me up for crack.*

Lilah's Learning Curve

You know I'm not the type
but my boyfriend said to try.
He told me I should flaunt it
so someone would want me—
so I kind of stuck out my hip
and this car stops.
The dude looked nervous
so that made two of us.
Maybe ten minutes
and he's done with his business.
It was almost too easy.
I think all men are crazy.
It's since then I've been afraid.
My boyfriend says, *What's so hard?*
Each time a guy's at the curb,
I'm thinking, is this one a cop?
And like I worry,
would my boyfriend ever hurt me?
In fact, sometimes I get so scared,
I forget about AIDS,
and then I'm in trouble
if the john won't use a rubber.
Or sometimes it's these old geezers
and you can't please them
which is tough
because they don't get off,

and they're panting,
and here you are thinking *9-1-1*
and *Who's gonna tell the guy's wife?*
And you kind of have to laugh
because you've tried like hell—
squeezing your ho-ho, holding his balls,
lifting your butt.
So you say something sweet
and at last the sucker comes,

and his cum is gummy
inside your thighs,
and after that, you wise up
and fire the pimp boyfriend
and double your price.

Soiled Doves

Low cooing under the alders,
scabby feet scrabbling in mud,
downy chests over their hearts,
and the constant gentle throb—
whom or what do they mourn,
these gray doves? Once
in another life I used to wear
muslin, I used to wear drab.
Out on the lake, white swans
swim in their zealous flotillas,
but if you ever dare mess
with a swan, you learn fast:
the pure nastiness of swans,
that orange and black beak.

Liesl in Queens, New York City, 1965

My neighbor Liesl sits on her brick porch,
bleached hair expensively permed.
Almost everyone on this block is Jewish,
or else Irish, and works for the fire department.
Under a clunky diamond bracelet,
the blue numbers are readable on her wrist.
The officers fed me. I was seventeen.
Did the officer select her right off the train?
Did he summon her from the women's barracks?
You wouldn't believe it, but I used to be pretty.
She yells at her fat kids:
Go, play in the traffic. There is no traffic.
Did she lift her skirt to service his needs
before or after he watched her eat?
Her lips look exactly like my lips
but her creamy lipstick is flaming red.
Every night she and her fireman husband
eat wide slabs of New York cheese cake,
and on Saturdays he plays the accordion.

(After World War II: Germany, Japan, USA:)

The German Lilli Cartoon Becomes the American Barbie doll

1.

A post-war German cartoon: blond, turned-up nose,
your perfect Aryan girl. Whatever Lilli did without
during the War, she plans never to go hungry again.
In the German cartoon: Lilli consults a fortune-teller
who predicts she'll meet someone handsome and rich.
Lilli's response: *Give me his phone number now.*
Same cartoon series: a policeman informs Lilli
it's illegal to wear a two-piece bikini.
Lilli asks the cop, *Which part shall I take off?*

2.

The Lilli series was such a hit, they made a Lilli doll
to sell as a pin-up in German tobacco shops,
a plaything for men, a gag-gift for their girlfriends.

3.

Enter an American, Ruth Handler, the co-owner
of Mattel toys and maker of breast prostheses—
who better to invent the well-stacked doll?
1959: Lilli is sent to Japan to be cast as Barbie,
from rigid plastic to injection-molded soft vinyl,
from a German whore to our all-American girl:
no nipples, no crack, a wardrobe to die for,
her eventual pink Corvette convertible,
and lots of little girls to worship her.

Lilli was a floozy, Lilli was a flirt.
When a man bought a Lilli doll,
he lifted up its skirt.

Automatic On-Line Translation from a Foreign Text I Can No Longer Locate on the Internet

> *—taken from an article about the "Comfort Women" forced to service Japanese soldiers during WWII*

"Since the mid-one-hundred-ninety-nine, Korean comfort women first time publicly accused the Japanese government.

"Comfort women have hidden memories of the past by their families after returning home is not accepted.

"Testimony from the parties, we can see where the pain and do not want people to know the bitterness.

"In her seventeenth spring of that year in northeast China have heard a good father to make money to take her.

"She entered the room and then locked up, and then she heard their father to see. She want to escape, but are surrounded by Japanese soldiers, flying wings hard.

"A soldier came to her and said "According to the command to do that!" Then ordered her clothes off.

"The next day began at half past eight, every thirty minutes to come in a soldier wearing a condom. Great generals wear no condoms.

"Day seven in the morning, the soldiers brought two Chinese people, saying that they were spies and their blindfolded, hands tied behind their backs, in front of them a ax blow. She can end up like them.

"Some of the men began drinking the morning, singing, in particular in the troops on the eve of excitement, is particularly brutal.

"Every time I see the Japanese flag, on the very resentment, no matter how much money to her can not make up her wounds."

Why Lillie Became a Prostitute—version six

He stood next to my bed
I'm your father
He slid under the covers
I was wearing my pj's with pandas.
I would never hurt you
He hurt me with his thing
Nothing happened
I don't remember any *thing*
I don't remember anything
I don't like pandas anymore

(Portland, Oregon, recently:)

After Great Pain

>   —*quoted from Ashly Lorenzana,*
>   Sex, Drugs & Being an Escort

I showed not one sign of any sort of pain.
I left it in the rooms I walked out of and away from.
And it was like finding some wounded animal
somewhere all alone and seeing that it was suffering great pain,
to remain beside it and cry at seeing it endure the hurt
and in the hope of your presence making it less afraid
as it lay there with your wounds
and it ended as the creature died beside you
marking the end of all its pain, and leaving you to walk away
with the memory of it that you won't ever forget,
and that you share with not one other being in time,
making you the loneliest only one that had been there
except for that thing which you watched die.

>   *Lillie was a jokester, Lillie was a card.*
>   *When I went to Lillie's house,*
>   *I'd never laughed so hard.*

Making the Beast with Two Backs, or how to be more vulgar than Iago

The discreet man will:
  test the mattress
  take a trip to the moon
  enjoy some horizontal refreshment
  take a turn on shooter's hill

The practical man will:
  get his oil changed
  get his ashes hauled
  get his wick dipped
  get his banana peeled
  get his kettle mended
  get his chimney swept out
  get his clock wound up
  get his broom dusted

The gross man will:
  do the bumpy ugly
  get more ass than a toilet
  have a bit of split mutton
  feed the bearded clam

But the poetic man, ah, the poetic man will:
  sheath the sword to the hilt
  bury the bishop
  ride the baloney pony
  give the ferret a run
  dance the blanket hornpipe
  give pussy a taste of cream
  drive the pink love bus into tuna town
  fidget the midget in Bridget

How to Deal with SWBS

> *—advice from Annie Sprinkle, retired prostitute
> and porn star, from* Whores and Other Feminists,
> *ed. Jill Nagle, 1997*

Admit that you are burned out.

>Hey, and who wouldn't be
>with some of these kids?
>
>And our principal takes
>the parents' side.

Take breaks and vacations.

>You know those sick days?
>We call them "mental health days."

Spend time in nature.

>The school smells of disinfectant.
>The adolescents reek of sweat.

Be in touch with your feelings.

>If I were anymore in touch with my feelings,
>I'd be screaming and kicking the floor.

Take good care of your body.

>Those kids are vectors:
>every germ in town.

If your SWBS is chronic, get the hell out of the business.

>I've worked in offices.
>I like my summers off.
>
>At least it's a job:
>what else would I do?

Oh-oh, says Annie, *you misunderstand me.*

>You mean it wasn't
SCHOOL workers burnout syndrome?
You mean it was SEX workers?
I say, *Same difference, better pay.*

In which the wife serves as the husband's emergency equipment

Sometimes I feel just like a toaster
permanently plugged into the kitchen wall
in case you happen to want toast.

Bye, bye, baby. I'm leaving you

cooked chicken, broccoli, and corn
in the refrigerator. You might want to melt
more cheese on the chicken casserole.
Just stick it in the microwave.

I'm leaving you

sorted socks,
clean clothes put away in drawers
and the shirts on their hangers.

I'm leaving you

because I don't want to be a toaster,
because I don't want to be toast,
because I'm starving on crumbs.

I'm leaving you

this one kiss under your pillow:
use it well.

(Any city in the United States before craigslist
stopped listing sexual services:)

craigslist

1. I am at least 18 years old.

Lilliana works at a Starbucks.
Customers admire her smile.
Sometimes she winks for tips
but she still can't make her rent.
She has dropped her art class
because it conflicts with her job.
Barista, Artiste, College Girl,
Lilliana rides two city buses
to get to the community college.
Monday on her way to class
she gave a dollar to the lady
pushing a shopping cart of rags.

2. I understand "women seeking men" may include adult content.

The shopping cart lady's quilt
lies bunched in the alley, yellow
and stained. Lilliana remembers
daisies and Queen Anne's lace
and how she and her little sister
lay crowned with daisy chains.
Lilliana was never an innocent:
even as a child she understood
how daisies could smell like pee.

3. I agree to flag as "prohibited" anything illegal or in violation of the craigslist <u>terms of use</u>.

She doesn't dare ask her parents
for one more handout or loan
because her parents already think

she's a fuck-up. The last time,
they made her sign a typed letter
promising to pay them every month
and even their no-strings handouts
come with advice. Maybe she *is*
a fuck-up. Maybe she's just fucked.

*4. By clicking on the links below, I release craigslist from any
liability that may arise from my use of this site.*

She can't believe how easy it is.
Why doesn't everyone do it?
One little ad and the men jump.

craigslist>personals>women seeking men

*Bright, attractive college girl who
can't afford to show you a good time.
I think I have it—what you need.*

They get the hint. It's like a date.
They both pretend. They are polite
and amazingly clean. It's hard work
playing Girlfriend. Some so shy,
so awkward, clumsy moves or none.
Others normal, even good-looking.

*5. It's NOT ok to contact this poster with services or other
commercial interests.*

And always these crisp new bills.
Do they go to the ATM before
or after they shower and shave?
Last night's guy had big red hands
that reeked of shoe polish. Her tits
still hurt. Does the guy milk cows?

*6. Choosing safer sex for you and your partner greatly reduces
the risk of contracting STDs including HIV—you can get*

answers to your <u>safer sex questions</u>, courtesy of staff members at the <u>SF city clinic</u>.

To celebrate paying the rent,
She skips her shift at Starbucks
and types up her term paper:
Women and Social Welfare.
Her parents do their weekly call:
*Lilliana dear, what do you want
for your birthday?* A retirement plan.
A gift certificate for Victoria's Secret.
A can of mace. *Books*, she tells them.
Barista, Student, Good Daughter.
She posts a new ad on craigslist
and waits. She can't bathe enough.

Tick-Tock, Time to Fuck

> If you have the time,
> I have the equipment.

DESIRE size 6 kinky beauty all day.

SINGLE Mom enjoys adult fling at short notice.

AIRPORT—Long layover? Phone Leah.

EROTIC mutual touch. For mature gents. Un-rushed.

CLASSY businesswoman by appointment.

44DD full service tonight.

GAY New to town. Available 24/7.

SEDUCTIVE lady, today only.

Leyesha is back. Call IMMEDIATELY.

LILLIAN busty bimbo, lunch special.

TEEN hottie for a happy ending - no sex 9am-3pm.

> Let the poor child sleep.
>
> Check your Rolex. Check your Timex.
> Someone sexy expects your call.

The Prostitute with the Heart of Gold

>   —Cosi Fabian, Whores and Other Feminists,
>   ed. Jill Nagle, 1997

Sufi proverb: *There is healing
in a woman's vagina*

Ishtar: *A prostitute compassionate
am I*

Prostitution as a service industry:
Is there anything more vulnerable

than a naked man with a hard-on?
asks a modern call girl.

Oh, surely there is: the limp droop.
Don't say I don't care.

*Will you be my girlfriend
for real?* he begs.

I promise him, yes,
that I will be for tonight.

>   *Lillie was the moonlight, Lillie was the stars.*
>   *When I went to Lillie's house,*
>   *she touched all my scars.*

(From a New Zealand newspaper, mid-December:)

The Classifieds Celebrate our Savior's Birth, Alleluia

*THE RED DOOR—Unwrap your Christmas present—
eager ladies waiting to tease and please.*

STRIPPERS Available for your Xmas functions.

LILY, a Christmas buffet of pure pleasure.

Hold your holiday STAG Night at the Dolls House.

Hold your holiday Hens Night at Dolls House.

*LEIA—sensual responsive and versatile
"Christmas Specials"*

NOËL's private dungeon, fetishes, mild to extreme.

*Men's Cruise Club. Watch Porn With Horny Guys
Sling   Orgyroom   Glory Holes   Sit on Santa's lap*

Open every day except Christmas.

>Have you been good this year?
>Have you been VERY good?
>Alleluia.

>*Lillie was my Christmas treat, Lillie was my toy.
>When I went to Lillie's house,
>I played like a big boy.*

Why Lillie Became a Prostitute—version seven

Whatever I tell you, you won't believe me:
I was a poor governess seduced by the son of a Lord
My mother was a procuress and sold my virginity
I was kidnapped, drugged, and gang-raped
I really love sex and can't get enough

Cosmetics, from *kosm'tikos,* skilled in arranging

> *from* kosmetos, *well-ordered*
> *from* kosmos, *order, the universe, the world*

I know how you women paint yourselves—
that cunning whore of Venice, the maiden blush.
I'll slip into the powder room to fix my face;
even Queen Elizabeth II carries lipstick in her purse.
The well-ordered cosmos requires that women
be beautiful and nubile, fecund and moist.

My daughter gave me a subscription to *Cosmo.*
It didn't make me young or sexy,

but let me tell you, baby,
you can waste a lot of money
on creams, on dreams.
Let me re-arrange the world for you.
That's what whores and goddesses
are hired to do.

> *Lillie was a beauty, Lillie was a jewel.*
> *When I went to Lillie's house,*
> *I hope I wasn't cruel.*

(In the middle of a long, happy marriage:)

In which this wife tells her husband the truth about sex in marriage

—in memory of Emma Goldman

I am tired of cooking dinner. Instead
I'd rather lick caterpillars just for the feel
of fur on each of my tongues.
I have one hundred slippery tongues
and each speaks a different dialect.
Is any one of them yours?
Often my breasts are annoyed
by the tedious fact that every penis
is an antenna.
These breasts are happy as owls
to dwell in a tree. Branches tremble
but they don't reach. Sometimes
I shed my camouflage skin. It sloughs
off in rainbows. Each color is a string
you must tune before you play me.
Your bow is a lightning streak.
Sometimes, though rarely, my body
is struck by lightning.
Other times I'm the best liar in Portland,
Oregon. Strangers have paid me
to lie. For you, my beloved,
I'll do it for free.

(In warm coastal waters and on my nature calendar:)

According to the Escort Agency's Calendar, November is Manatee Awareness Month

All year long I swim among them,
our gray flippers like large paddles,

and our perfect breasts
bobbing beneath the shallow water.

We belong to the order *Serena*
because sailors mistake us for mermaids.

Some men are so lonesome or so hungry
they are willing to drown.

As we graze in warm saltwater bays
on algae, mangrove, and water hyacinths,

we squeak and whistle to tell our calves
I love you I love you

When you pay us, you may not believe
most of us used to be human.

Lillie was a dolphin, Lillie was a wave.
When I went to Lillie's house,
I was lying on her grave.

Deathless Aphrodite of the Spangled Mind

Foam-born Aphrodite
Gold-crowned Aphrodite
Dark-eyed Aphrodite
Silver-footed Aphrodite
Aphrodite of the Beautiful Buttocks
Laughter-loving Aphrodite

She who Postpones Old Age

Aphrodite, in your service
see how I have grown old.
The elders turn from me in pity,
the young men turn from me in scorn.
My breasts lie empty and flat
on my bony ribs,
but my lips still remember
how I brought men to pleasure.
Bring me a blind man
with a wrinkled member.
Lay him down on my golden couch.
Now and forever, watch how we sparkle.

About the Author

Penelope Scambly Schott, author of a novel and several books of poetry, was awarded four New Jersey arts fellowships before moving to Oregon where her verse biography *A is for Anne: Mistress Hutchinson Disturbs the Commonwealth* received an Oregon Book Award for Poetry. Individual poems have appeared in *APR, Georgia Review, Nimrod*, and elsewhere.

Penelope has enjoyed fellowships at the Fine Arts Work Center in Provincetown, Massachusetts, the Vermont Studio Center in Johnson, Vermont, and the Wurlitzer Foundation in Taos, New Mexico.

Professionally, she has sold cosmetics at Macy's in Herald Square, made donuts at Scrumpy's cider mill, taken care of old people as a certified home health aide, worked as an artist's model, and—as punishment for her Ph.D. in Late Medieval English literature—spent years and years teaching college literature and creative writing courses.

Penelope lives with her husband and their dog in Portland, Oregon where she hosts a series of poetry salons—although she and the dog have an alternate life during which they spend part of each week in the small wheat-growing town of Dufur where she teaches an annual poetry workshop. From her Dufur house, Penelope can see the east side of Mount Hood, the high school football scoreboard, and the Milky Way.

Bibliography

Melvin R. Adams, *Netting the Sun: A Personal Geography of the Oregon Desert*, Washington State University, Pullman, Washington, 2001.

Alexa Albert, *Brothel: Mustang Ranch and Its Women*, Ballantine Books, New York, 2001.

Anonymous, personal interviews, 2009-2011.

Jacqueline Baker Barnhart, *The Fair but Frail: Prostitution in San Francisco 1849-1900*, University of Nevada Press, Reno, Nevada, 1986.

Kay Reynolds Blair, *Ladies of the Lamplight*, Western Reflections Publishing Company, Montrose, Colorado, 2004.

Anne M. Butler, *Daughters of Joy, Sisters of Misery: Prostitutes in the American West 1865-90*, University of Illinois Press, Urbana and Chicago, Illinois, 1985.

Hilary Evans, *Harlots, Whores & Hookers: A History of Prostitution*, Dorset Press, New York, 1979.

Anna Griffin, "Walking Away from 82nd Avenue," *The Oregonian*, Portland, Oregon, February 4, 2010.

Julie Roy Jeffrey, *Frontier Women: "Civilizing" the West? 1840-1880*, rev. edition, Hill and Wang, New York, 1998.

Ruth Mazo Karras, *Common Women: Prostitution and Sexuality in Medieval England*, Oxford University Press, New York and Oxford, 1996.

Stewart Holbrook, ed. Brian Booth, *Wildmen, Wobblies & Whistle Punks: Stewart Holbrook's Lowbrow Northwest*, Oregon State University Press, Corvallis, Oregon, 1992.

M.G. Lord, *Forever Barbie: The Unauthorized Biography of a Real Doll*, Walker and Company, New York, 1994, 2004.

Ashly Lorenzana, *Sex, Drugs & Being an Escort*, Lulu, n.d.

Gary and Gloria Meier, *Those Naughty Ladies of the Old Northwest*, Maverick Publications, Bend, Oregon, 1990.

Jay Moynahan, *Prostitute Dictionary of the Old West*, 3rd Edition, Chickadee Publishing, Spokane, Washington, 2007.

Jay Moynahan, *Remedies from the Red Lights: Cures, Treatments and Medicines from the Sportin' Ladies of the Frontier West*, Chickadee Publishing, Spokane, Washington, 2000.

Jill Nagle, ed., *Whores and Other Feminists*, Routledge, New York, 1997.

Ruth Rosen, *The Lost Sisterhood: Prostitution in America, 1900-1918*, Johns Hopkins University Press, Baltimore, Maryland, 1982.

Michael Rutter, *Upstairs Girls: Prostitution in the American West*, Farcountry Press, Helena, Montana, 2005.

Anne Seagraves, *Soiled Doves: Prostitution in the Early West*, Wesanne Publications, Hayden, Idaho, 1994.

Sin in the Sagebrush, Exhibit at the High Desert Museum, Bend, Oregon, 2010.

Rick Steber, *Women of the West*, Tales of the Wild West, Volume 5, Bonanza Publishing, Prineville, Oregon, 1988.

Merlin Stone, *When God Was a Woman*, Harcourt Brace Jovanovich, New York, 1978.

Diane Wolkstein and Samuel Kramer, *Inanna: Queen of Heaven and Earth*, Harper and Row, New York, 1983.

www.urbanslang.com

Other Recent Titles from Mayapple Press:

Nola Garrett, *The Pastor's Wife Considers Pinball,* 2013
    Paper, 74pp, $14.95 plus s&h
    ISBN 978-1-936419-16-6

Marjorie Manwaring, *Search for a Velvet-Lined Cape,* 2013
    Paper, 94pp, $15.95 plus s&h
    ISBN 978-1-936419-15-9

Edythe Haendel Schwartz, *A Palette of Leaves,* 2012
    Paper, 74pp, $14.95 plus s&h
    ISBN 978-1-936419-14-2

Sarah Busse, *Somewhere Piano,* 2012
    Paper, 72pp, $14.95 plus s&h
    ISBN 978-1-936419-13-5

Betsy Johnson-Miller, *Fierce This Falling,* 2012
    Paper, 72pp, $14.95 plus s&h
    ISBN 978-1-936419-12-8

William Heyen, *Straight's Suite for Craig Cotter and Frank O'Hara,* 2012
    Paper, 86pp, $14.95 plus s&h
    ISBN 978-1-936419-11-1

Lydia Rosner, *The Russian Writer's Daughter,* 2012
    Paper, 104pp, $15.95 plus s&h
    ISBN 978-1-936419-10-4

John Palen, *Small Economies,* 2012
    Paper, 58pp, $13.95 plus s&h
    ISBN 978-1-936419-09-8

Susan Azar Porterfield, *Kibbe,* 2012
    Paper, 62pp, $14.95 plus s&h
    ISBN 978-1-936419-08-1

Susan Kolodny, *After the Firestorm,* 2011
    Paper, 62pp, $14.95 plus s&h
    ISBN 978-1-936419-07-4

Eleanor Lerman, *Janet Planet,* 2011
    Paper, 210pp, $16.95 plus s&h
    ISBN 978-1-936419-06-7

George Dila, *Nothing More to Tell,* 2011
    Paper, 100pp, $15.95 plus s&h
    ISBN 978-1-936419-05-0

For a complete catalog of Mayapple Press publications, please visit our website at *www.mayapplepress.com*. Books can be ordered direct from our website with secure on-line payment using PayPal, or by mail (check or money order). Or order through your local bookseller.